AF605156

SYDNEY

First published in 2025 by New Holland Publishers
Sydney, Australia.
newhollandpublishers.com

 A record of this book is held at the National Library of Australia.

ISBN: 9781760797782

Managing Director: Fiona Schultz
General Manager/Publisher: Olga Dementiev
Designer: Andrew Davies
Production Director: Arlene Gippert
Printed in China

Other titles by New Holland.

SYDNEY

Marriott

154

PARK

40

AXA AUSTRALIA

FISHBURN
Transport
Sydney Ferries

NSW
Transport
FRESHWATER
SYDNEY

FLATS

MANLY SAILING

L100

15
NO STOPPING

Westfield

UGG
UGG
Dr. Seuss
OROTON
OROTON

NO
TURN

VICTORIA

FOUR SEASONS HOTEL
GALLERIA
155

L. MACQUARIE ESQ

seum of
Contemporary
Art

A.S.N.C.
A.S.N.C.

XV
XIV

King Street Wharf
Aquarium Wharf
Cockle Bay Wharf
Harbourside
ICC Sydney

AUSTRALIAN MUSEUM

ART GALLERY OF NEW SOUTH WALES
GIOTTO

CANOVA
JEAN GOUJON

154

1920

HSBC

King St No 5
MA STIC CRUISES
SYDNEY SHOWBOATS
5

DOYLES
Doyles

NO WAVES

25

- Sydney is the **capital** of New South Wales, and was the original site of the establishment of a colony in 1788.
- **George Street** is the oldest street in Sydney.
- Sydney is one of the most **multicultural** cities in the world, and one-third of residents speak a language other than English.
- The city is among the top fifteen most-visited in the world and has over **3 million tourists** visit Sydney annually.
- Sydney's nickname is '**Sin City**'.
- Those who were born and live in Sydney are known as **Sydneysiders**.
- In summer, **cricket** is the most popular sport in Sydney and in Australia.
- The **Sydney Mint** is the oldest remaining public building in Sydney, built between 1811 and 1816. **Cadmans Cottage** is the oldest house still existing, built in 1816 located in The Rocks area.
- The **Royal Botanical Gardens** has 30 hectares of beautiful gardens and plants.

- The **Sydney Harbour Bridge** is the widest long-span bridge and the tallest steel arch bridge in the world.
- The Sydney Harbour Bridge is nicknamed '**The Coat Hanger**'.
- The **Sydney Opera House** is 185 metres long and 120 metres wide and is World Heritage-listed.
- The original cost estimate to build Sydney Opera House was $7 million. The final cost was **$102 million** and took **14 years** to build.
- **Queen Elizabeth II** opened the Sydney Opera House on 20 October 1973.
- Over **15,000 light bulbs** are changed every year at the Sydney Opera House.
- **Crown Sydney** at Barangaroo stands 271 metres tall.
- Sydney has over 100 beaches. The longest, **Lady Robinsons Beach**, is five kilometres long.
- **Bondi Beach** is one of the world's most famous beaches and is a popular hot spot for visitors.
- The suburb of **Point Piper** is considered to be the most expensive and exclusive place to live in Sydney.
- A light art show is an annual event in Sydney between May and June called **Vivid Sydney** and offers a spectacular light show featuring the Sydney Harbour Bridge and the Sydney Opera House.